NATIONAL GEOGRAPHIC

Our Clubhouse

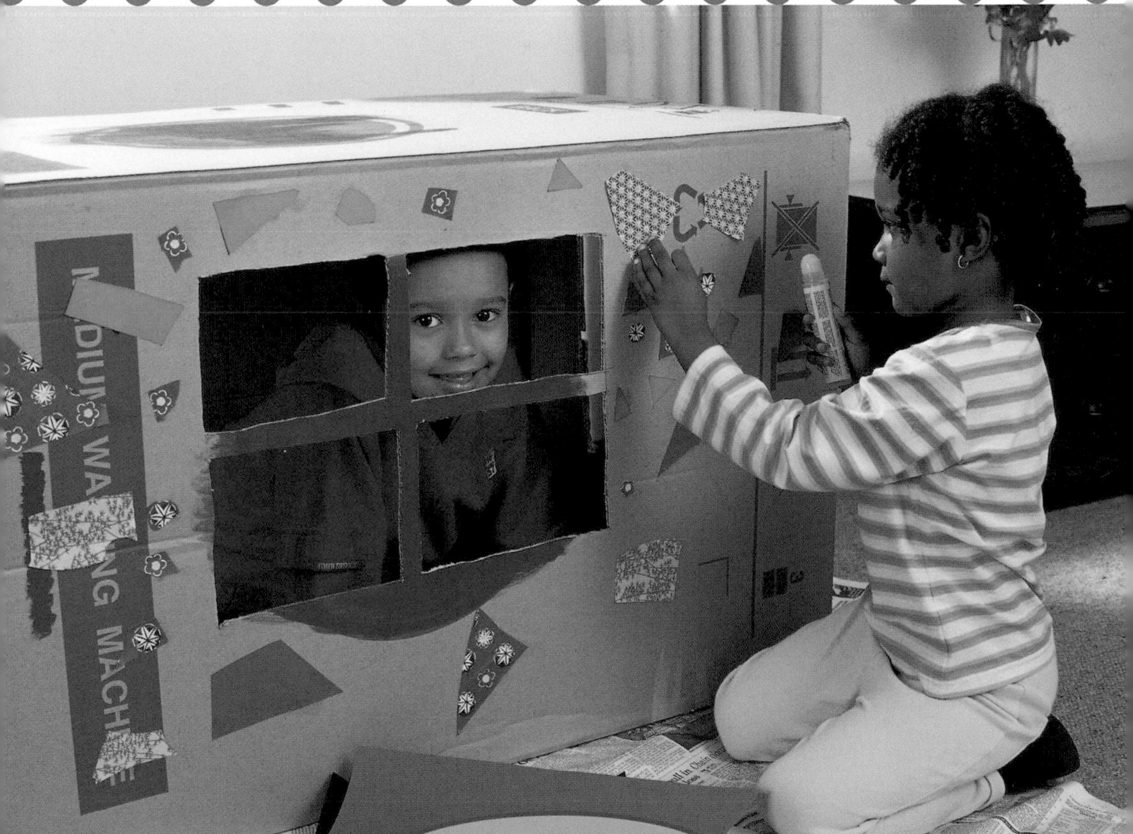

Mark Macey

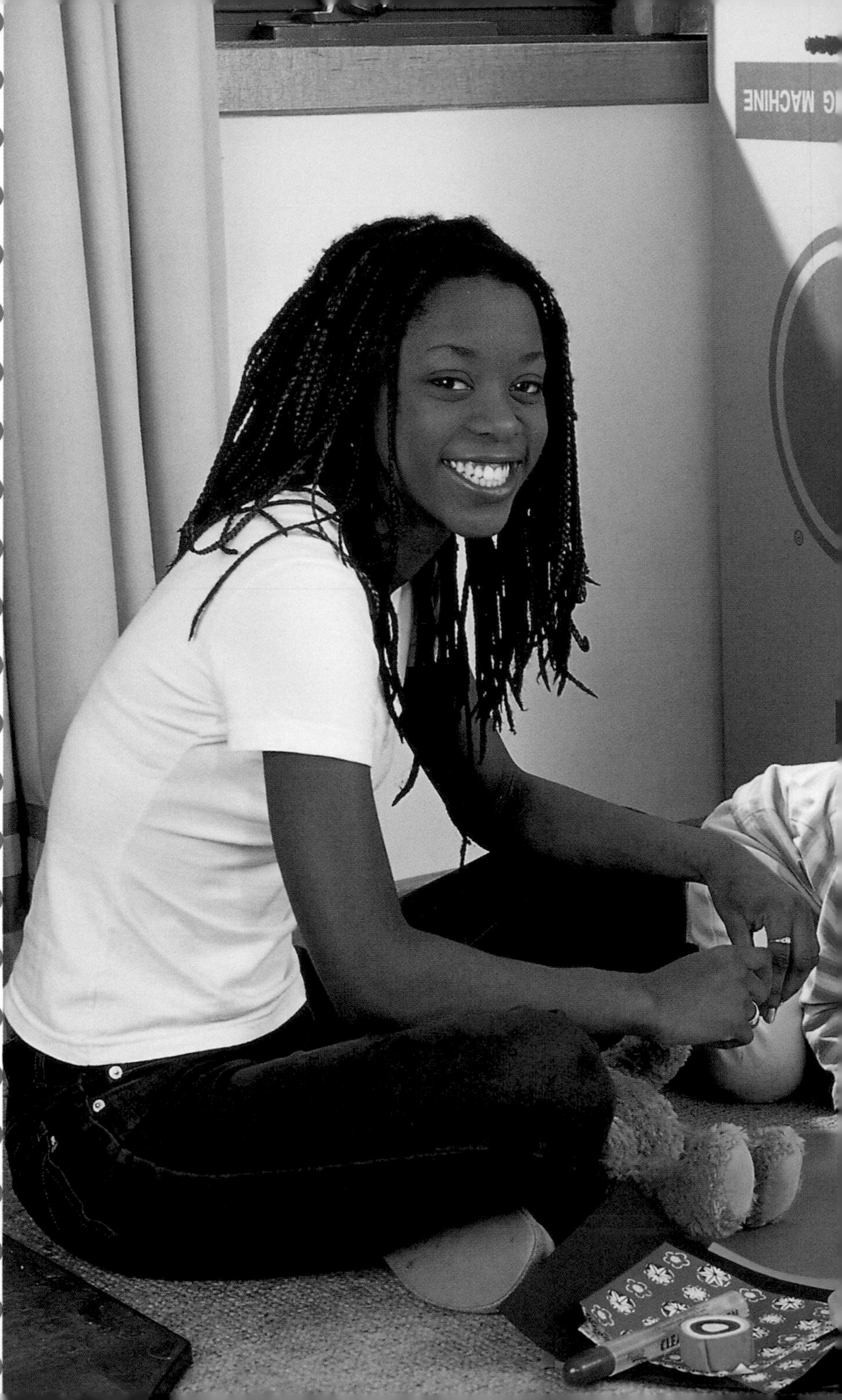

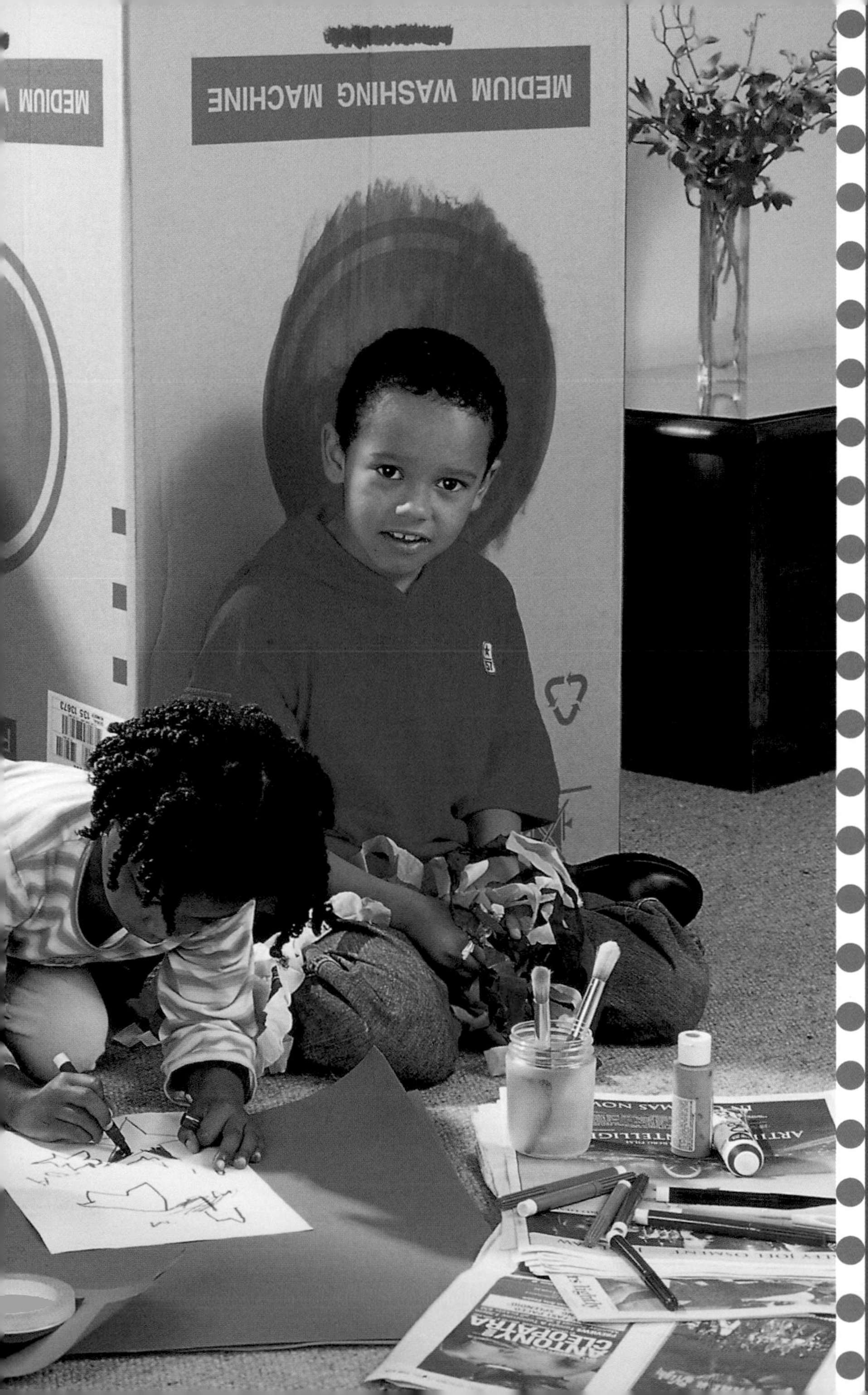
MEDIUM WASHING MACHINE

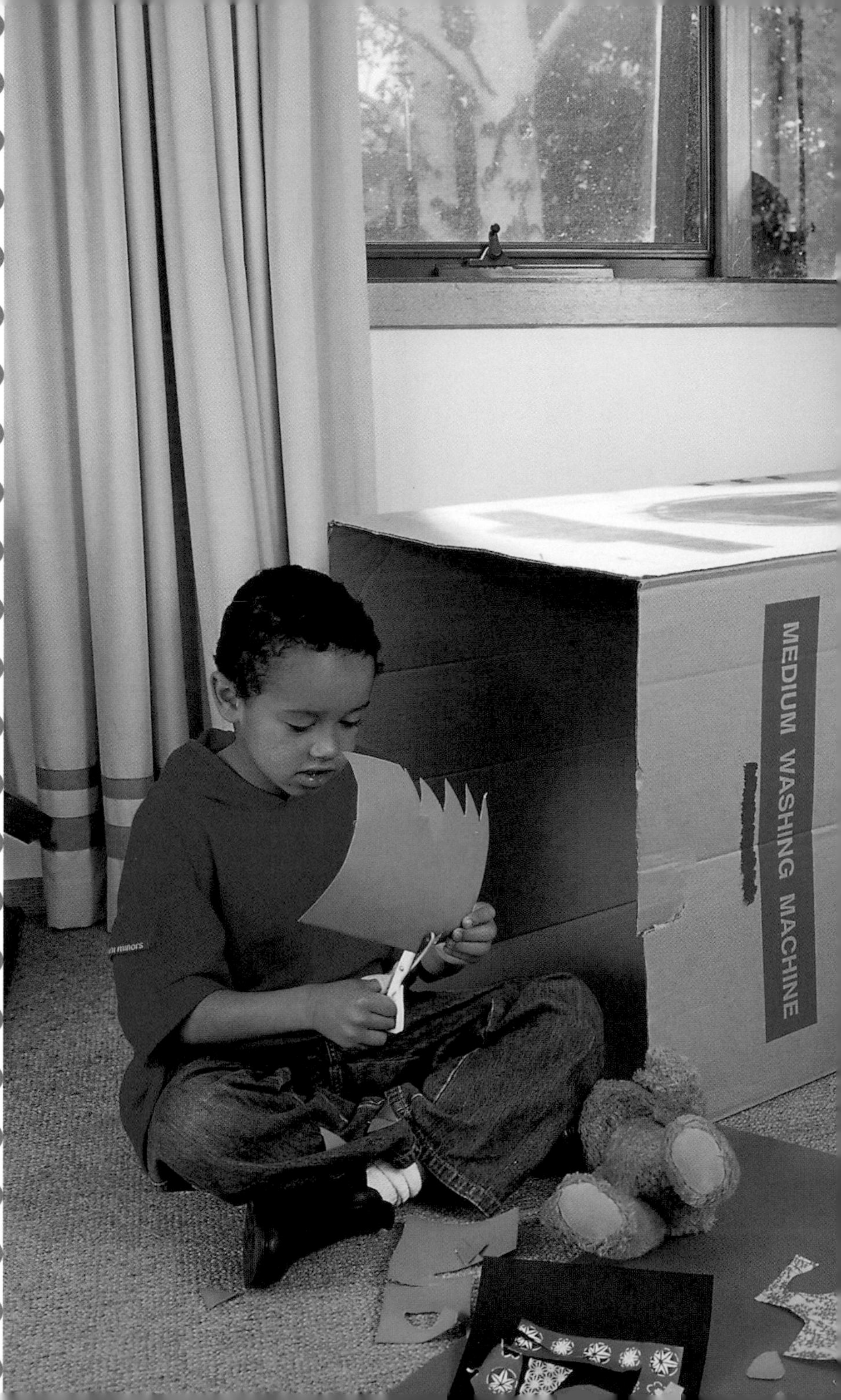
MEDIUM WASHING MACHINE

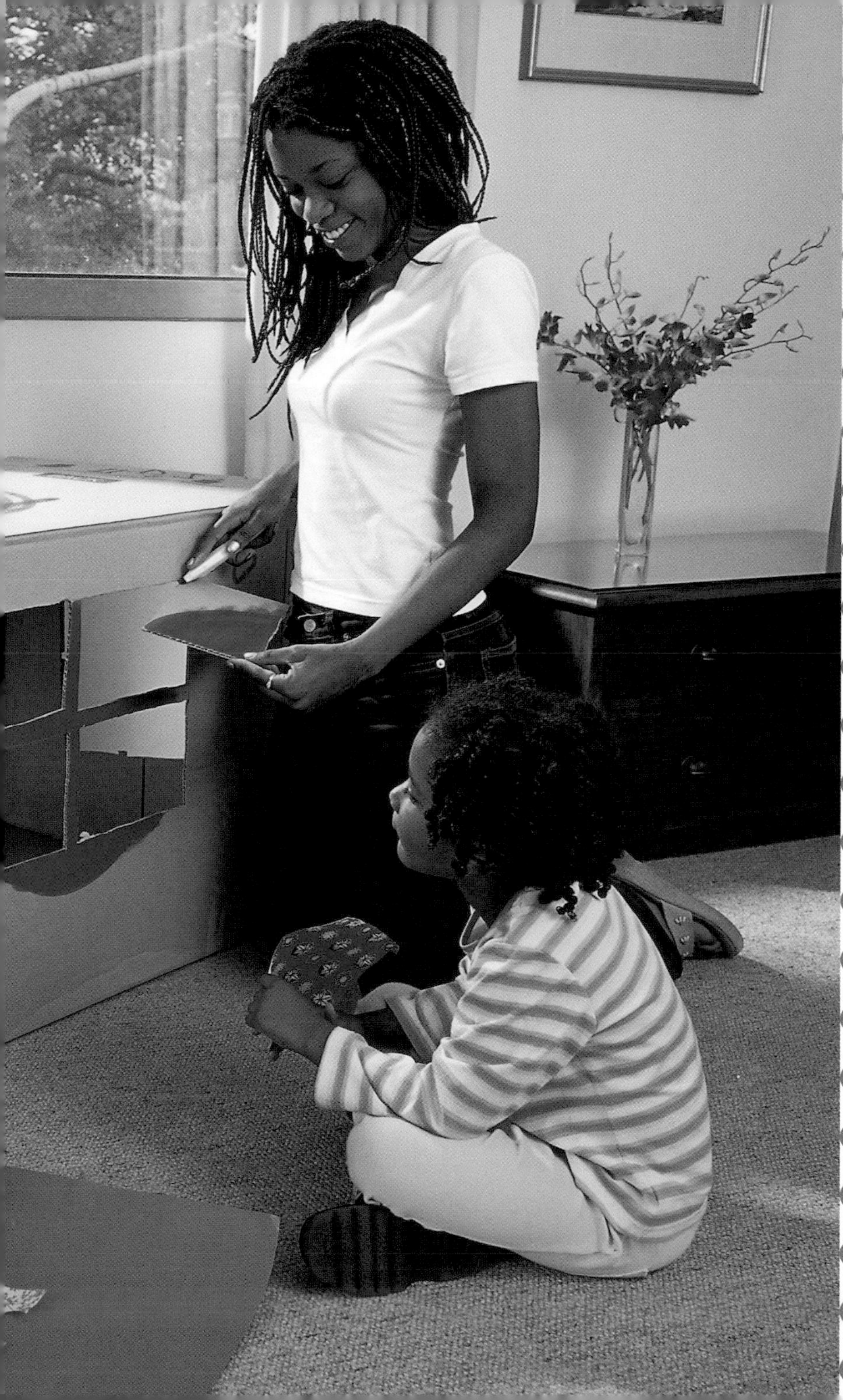

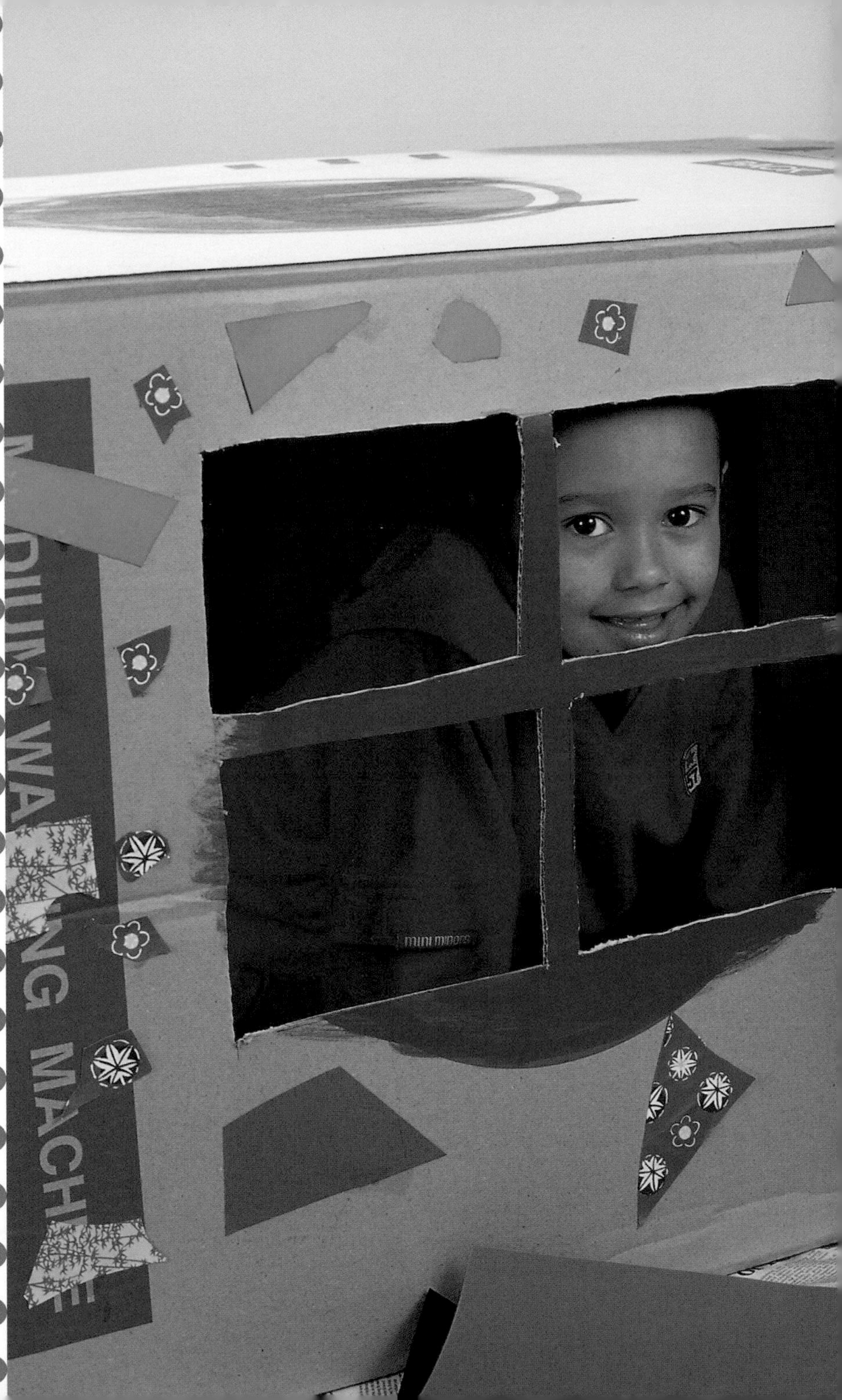

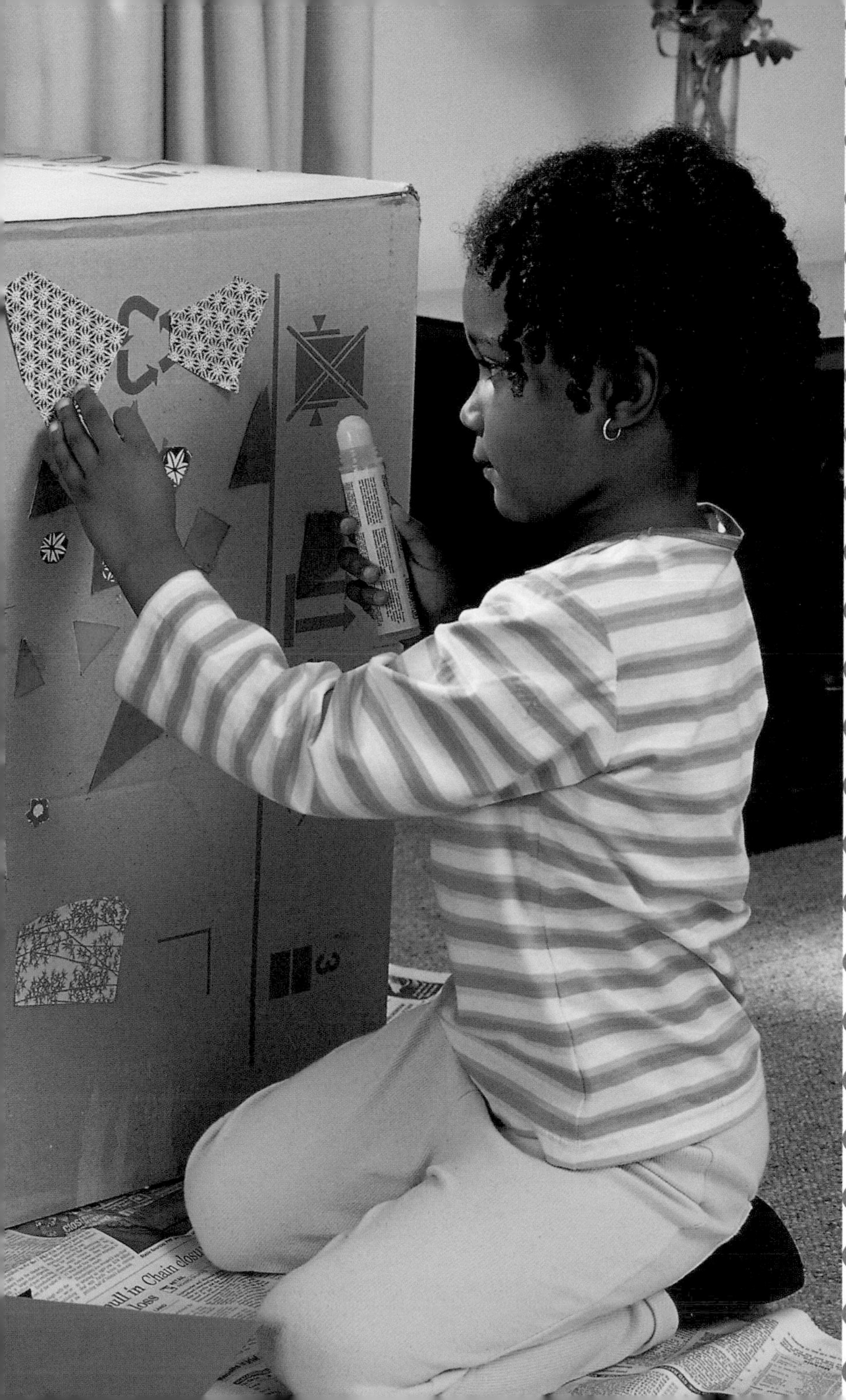

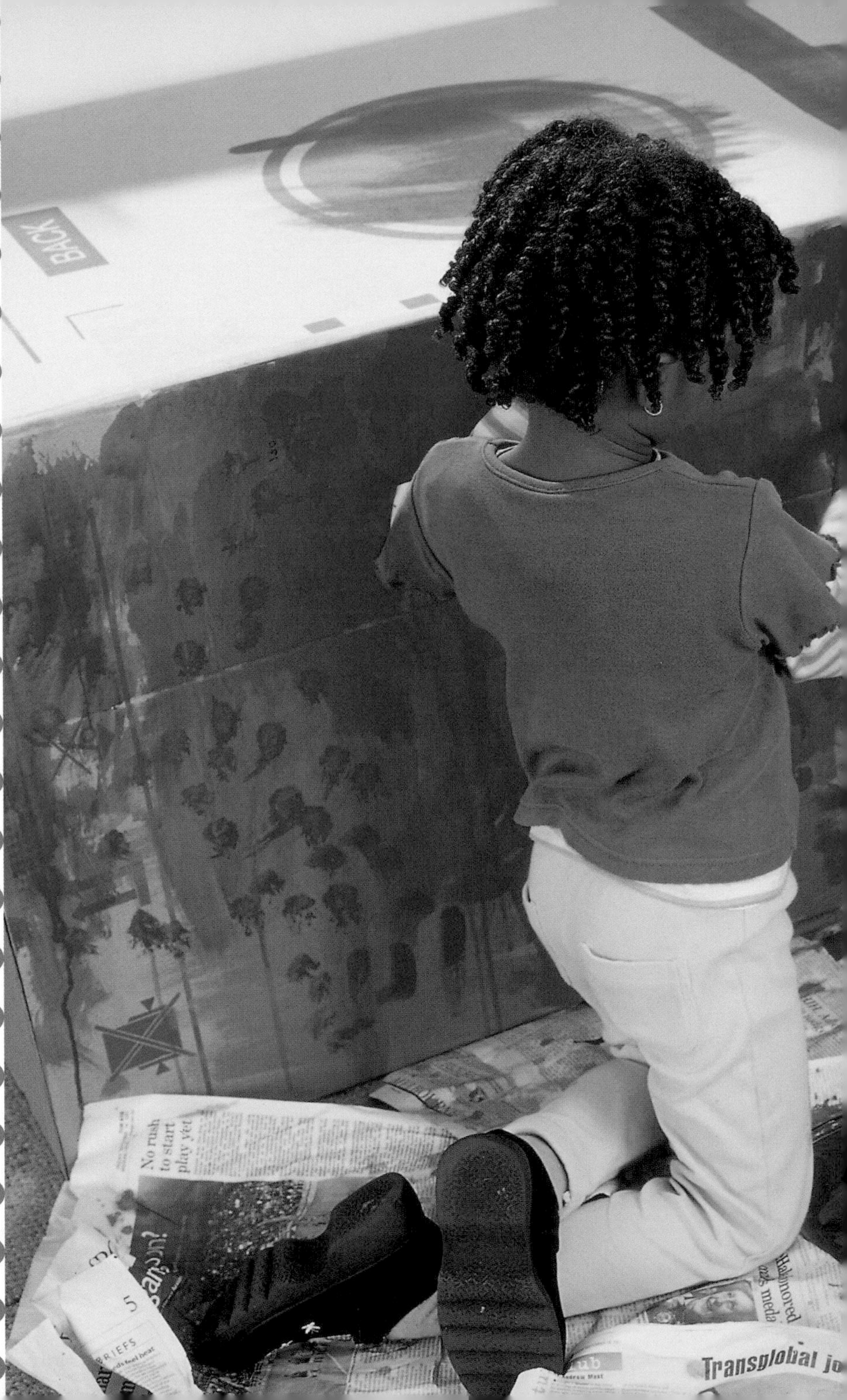
BACK
No rush to start play yet

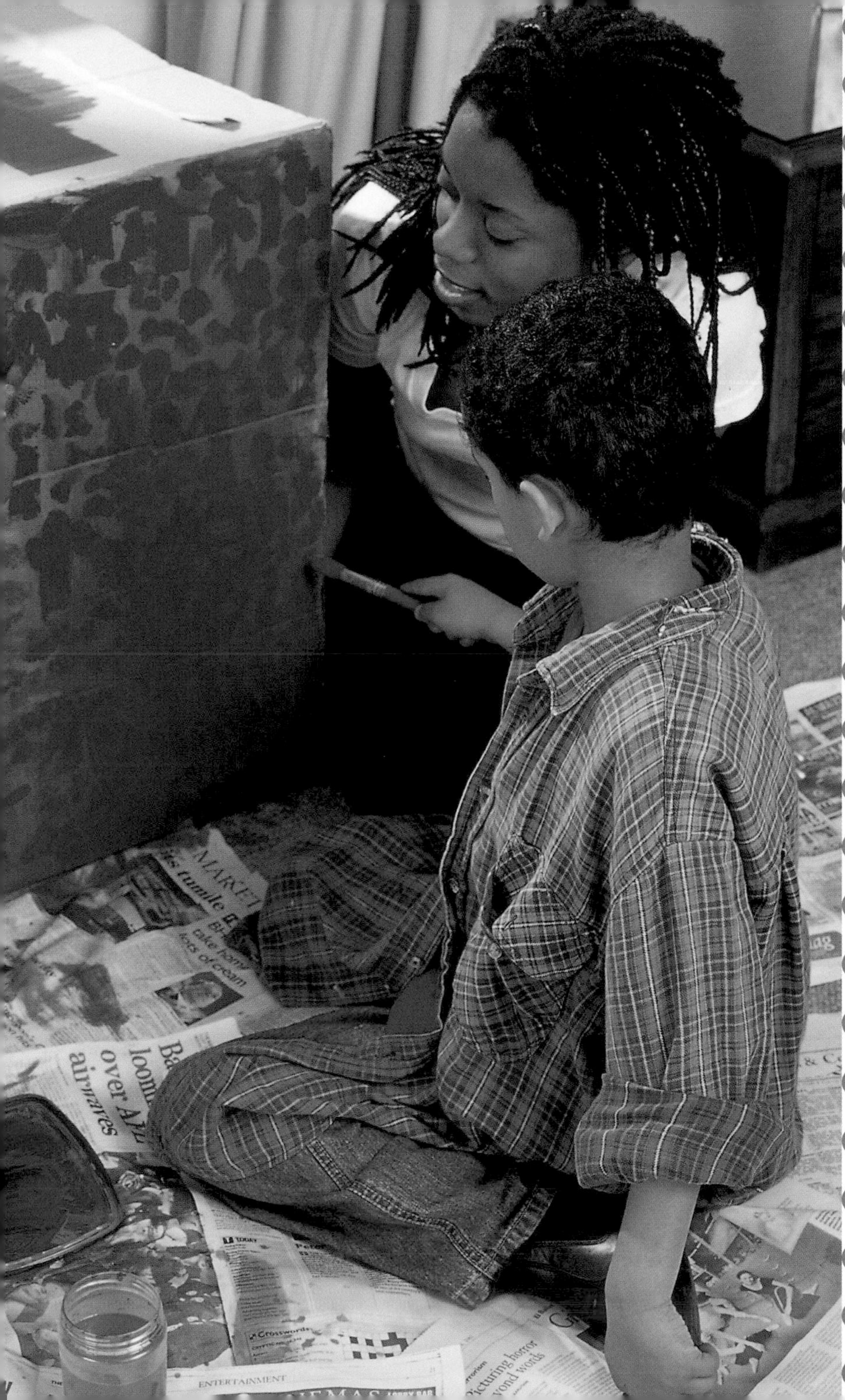
take home
lots of cream
over
airwaves
ENTERTAINMENT
Picturing horror
Crosswords

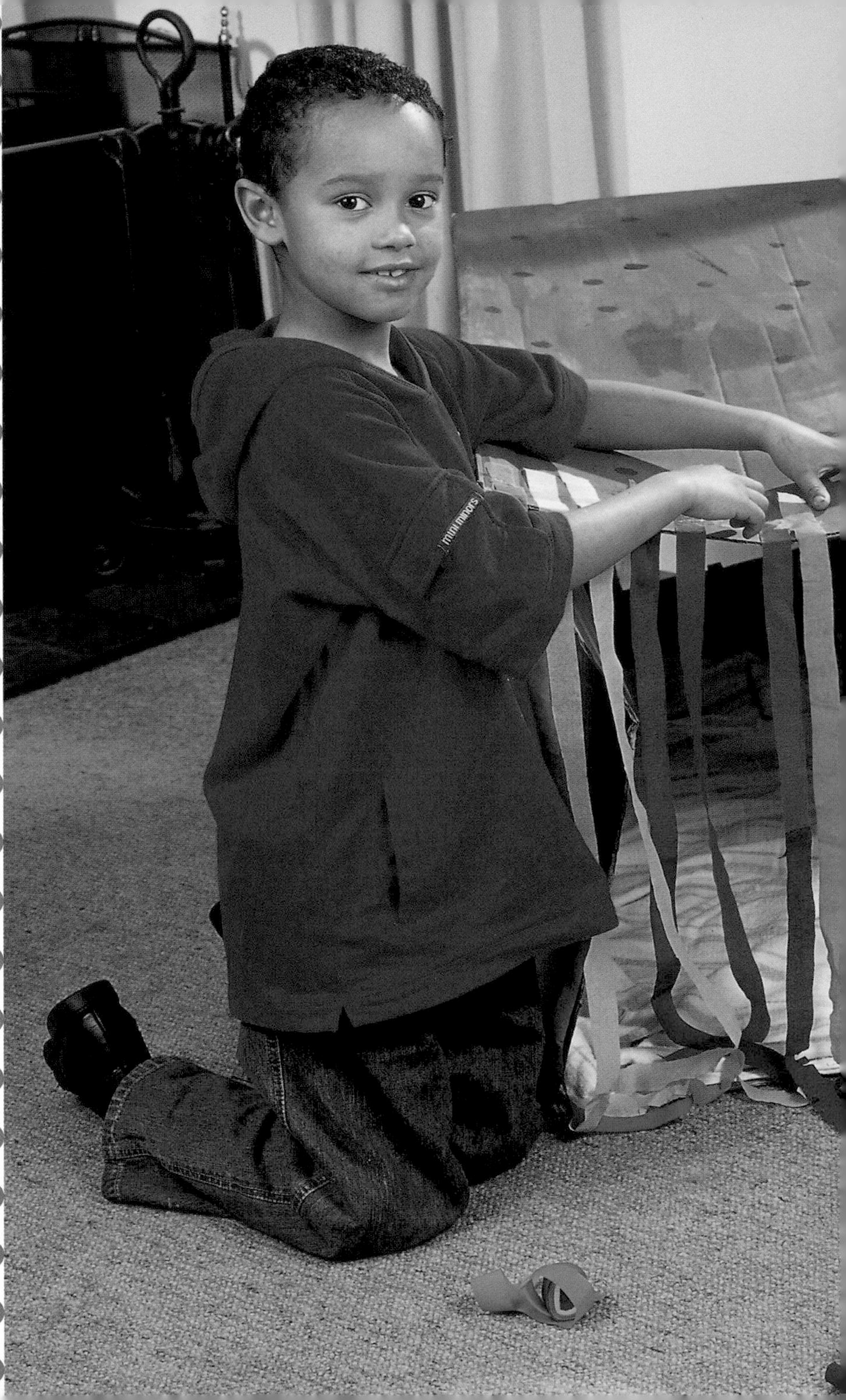

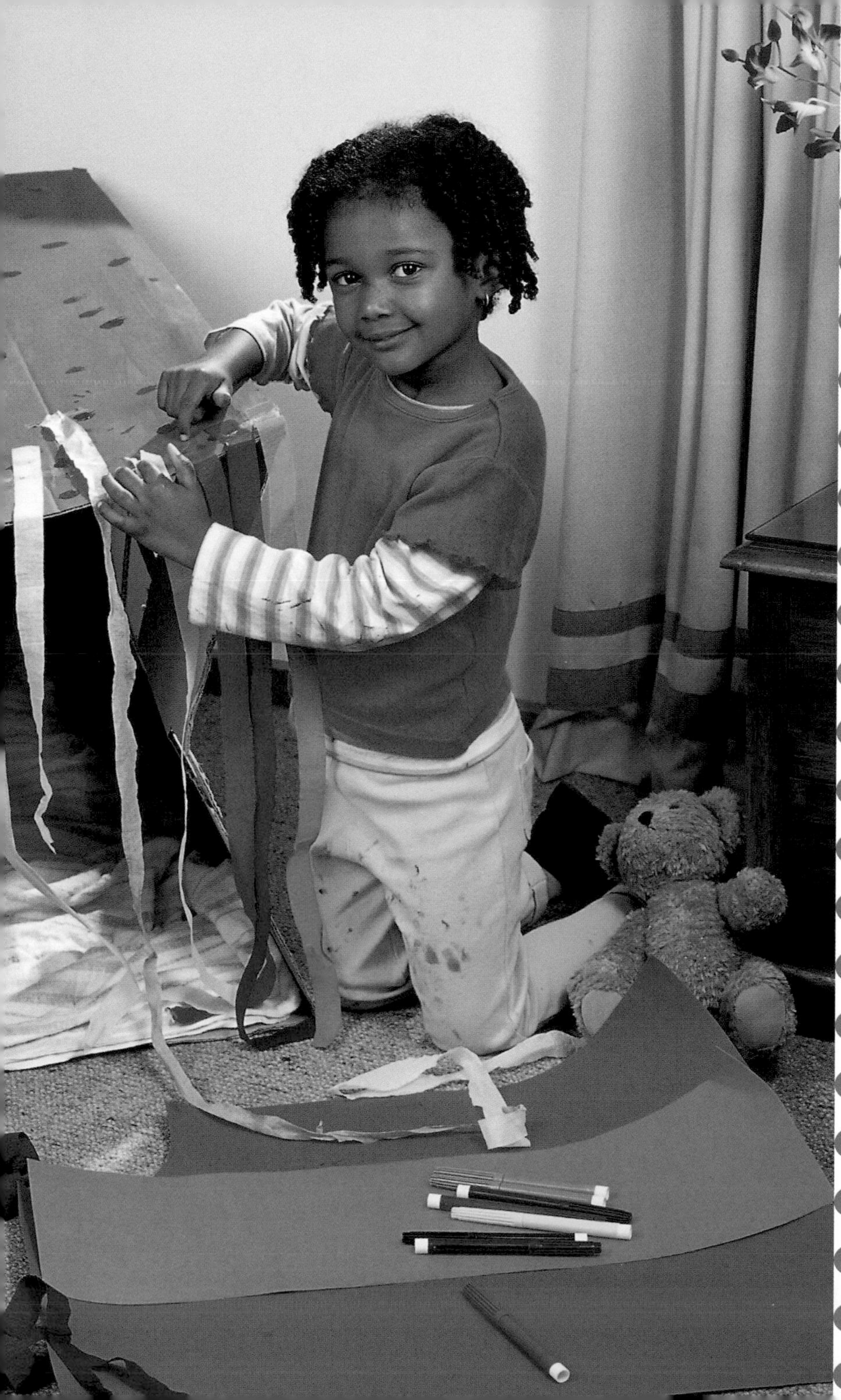

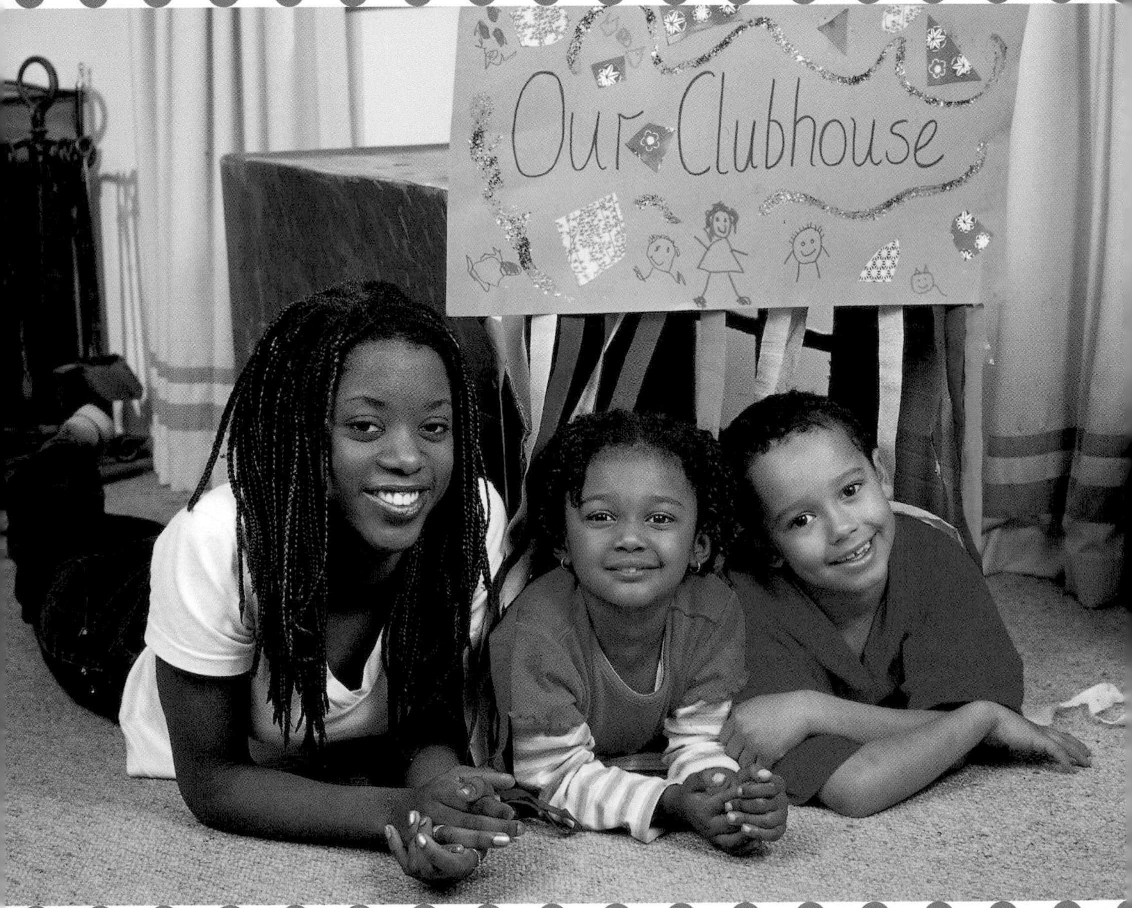
Our Clubhouse